THOMAS E. FRENCH

Remembrances and Recollections of World War II

Published by XN3 Technologies

Copyright © 2025 by The French Family

All rights reserved. No part of this publication may be reproduced, stored or transmitted in any form or by any means, electronic, mechanical, photocopying, recording, scanning, or otherwise without written permission from the publisher. It is illegal to copy this book, post it to a website, or distribute it by any other means without permission.

Cover image: Into the Jaws of Death, June 6, 1944, by Robert F. Sargent (U.S. Coast Guard/National Archives). U.S. 1st Infantry Division disembarking from a Coast Guard-manned LCVP (Landing Craft, Vehicle, Personnel).

All other images, unless otherwise noted, are courtesy of the French Family.

First edition

ISBN (paperback): 9798275144161
ISBN (hardcover): 979-8-9998792-3-3

Contents

Editorial Note		iv
1	Part 1: Induction and Arrival at Camp Grant	1
2	Part 2: Basic Training at Camp Fannin, Texas	4
3	Part 3: Deployment: Fort Meade to Scotland	8
4	Part 4: Arrival in England and Joining the 1st Infantry...	11
5	Part 5: D-Day: The Omaha Beach Landing and Advance Inland	15
6	Part 6: Operation COBRA and the Fight for Marigny	23
7	Part 7: The Breakout and the Argentan-Falaise Pocket	27
8	Part 8: Advance into Belgium and the Siegfried Line	30
9	Part 9: The Battle for Aachen and Hand-to-Hand Combat	33
10	Part 10: Wounded, AWOL in Paris, and Court Martial	35
11	Part 11: Hurtgen Forest, the Battle of the Bulge, and Hill...	42
12	Part 12: Wounded Again on Hill 587	50
13	Part 13: Recovery in England	54
14	Part 14: The Voyage Home on the Queen Elizabeth	57
15	Part 15: Transport to Texas and Furlough Home	60
16	Part 16: Rehabilitation at Beaumont General Hospital	64
17	Part 17: Final Transfer and Discharge	67
Photographs		70

Editorial Note

The personal experiences shared in this book were originally handwritten by the author on a paper notepad. The contents of that handwritten paper notepad was then typed into a computer word-processor, and then printed and bound with spiral binding. The spiral-bound copies were distributed by members of the French Family to the extended family.

This book is produced from a scan of a spiral bound copy. The original spelling, grammar, and punctuation is reproduced in this book exactly with only a few minor corrections of typos.

The original text was not split into parts. This book has been split seventeen different parts based on the subject content of each part.

1

Part 1: Induction and Arrival at Camp Grant

I was 18 years old on August 23, 1943. A few days later I received my notice to appear for a pre-induction physical exam. I had volunteered for the Army Air Corps before my birthday with the hope of becoming a bombardier. There were several from my high school senior class hoping to join the Army Air Corps or the Navy Air Corps. There were quite a few of us from Columbia County, Wisconsin that day, in the first part of September, to receive our physicals. We loaded onto two buses in Portage bound for Milwaukee where our exams were to take place. I passed with flying colors, except for my eyes, which kept me out of the Army Air Corps. Because of this I settled for the Army. All of us who were going into the Army, Navy, or whatever were inducted that day, then sent back on the buses to Portage to spend a few days at home before being called into service.

Toward the end of September we received our call to active duty. We again went to Portage to board the buses for Camp Grant, Illinois which is near Rockford. At Camp Grant we traded civvies for Army uniforms and began our indoctrination into the ways of the Army. We were now introduced to reveille, fall out to morning formation and roll-call, fall out to formation to march to the chow hall, chow-lines, Army food, Army haircuts, shots, inspections, how to make up Army bunks, Army training films, bed checks, taps, and lights out! During this time we attended lectures on the way we were to conduct ourselves and to respect authority, be it Officers or non-comms. It seems as though we spent all day falling into formation, marching somewhere, then falling out of formation again. By the time that taps sounded we were ready to settle down and go to sleep.

Soon a week had gone by and we were marching in formation with packs on our backs, the packs now contained everything that we owned because our civilian clothes had been sent home. As soon as we could march with our packs, we headed for the train which was to take us to a new destination for Basic Training; this turned out to be Camp Fannin, Texas which is about half way between Kilgore and Tyler, Texas. I knew several of the fellows that were in the same car on the train with me because they were from Portage: "Don (Moe) Markofski," or Pardeeville: "LaVern Dolajack," Jim Fladd was from Madison, one was my PE Instructor from Portage High School. One was about my age from Waterloo, Iowa, one was also about my age from Rockford, Illinois and there were three older fellows, all married from Milwaukee.

We ate, slept, and played cards most of the way into Kilgore except when we were watching the new type of scenery as we were coming closer to Kilgore. At Kilgore we marched from the train to waiting buses for the trip to Camp Fannin. Kilgore is an oil town, with oil derricks all over. This was really something different for all of us. We arrived at Camp Fannin, what a rude awakening for us! This camp had been thrown together in a minimum amount of time. Originally Fannin was to be an Army air field but the winds were so bad at times that it was difficult to land their planes here. The winds were so ferocious that 8×8 posts had been driven into the ground, three on each side of our one story barracks, with steel cables running from the eves of the building down to the posts.

We were all curious about this setup, but we were told to wait until the winds started blowing, then we would understand. East Texas has bad storms at times: rain, hail, wind, and tornadoes!

2

Part 2: Basic Training at Camp Fannin, Texas

Our first week in Camp Fannin was good weather-wise, but not so good for us. We were in for 17 weeks of basic training with calisthenics, obstacle courses, more shots, more training films, more inspections, rifle training, marching in "close order drill," bayonet drill, rifle disassembly & assembly including learning the names of all of the parts, hand grenade training, machine gun training, map reading, and long marches with field packs and rifles. We now carried our rifles all of the time except to the Mess Hall.

During our first 6 weeks of Basic Training, our only break was an occasional evening at the PX for an hour or so. On Sunday afternoons we were usually free to spend two or three hours at the PX for a beer or a quart of ice cream while we listened to the juke box. We missed our music because we were not allowed any radios in our barracks at that particular time. After six weeks, we were allowed Saturday night passes if we passed the weekly inspection on Saturday morning, or if we were not on KP duty.

After six weeks our combat training started in earnest. We started going to the rifle range to fire our rifles, and the range where we threw live hand grenades. We fired mortars, practiced hand to hand combat, and learned how to use our bayonets on dummies. We also had longer marches, and speed marches of from five to seven miles where we marched five minutes, then ran five minutes, then marched five minutes, etc. Full field inspections were also started, which included everything we now owned, laid out on a blanket in front of our tents in the field.

Next there were gas mask drills. For this we put on our gas masks adjusting the straps to conform to our faces, then we had to go into a building filled with gas, stand around for a few minutes then take the mask off and run for the door. Of course there was always a mad rush for the door that was the only exit from the building and a fight almost always broke out at the exit because our eyes were burning so that we could hardly see.

Then there was the infiltration course. Here we crawled under barbed wire carrying our rifles while machine guns fired over us with live ammo. We also learned how to use the Army compass for daytime and nighttime use. We were then taken out in small groups, finding our way from one area to another with a map and the compass. We had an advanced obstacle course to go through also. This included walking on a log over a stream, crawling under barbed wire, walking through a muddy area, climbing a high wall, going hand-over-hand on a steel bar over a small ravine, etc., until we returned to the stream, this time to swing on a rope across it and drop off on the other side, then we had to run about a mile to the finish line. Our reward, we were allowed to do this at least twice each week until the last week of basic training.

The days did fly by very fast, Thanksgiving passed by and I barely remember it. Soon the weather turned cold and rainy as it neared Christmas. The parade ground that had been almost as hard as concrete turned to mud. We now marched with our raincoats on and our rifles turned with the barrels down so they would not fill up with water and ice. We spent much of our time cleaning our shoes and equipment, but the training went on. I caught a cold and sore throat but didn't go to the dispensary because I wanted to finish Basic the first time around! I spent every day that I could at Christmas time sleeping and relaxing and eating. We had great food at the Mess Hall, turkey and ham with all the trimmings. We also shared the packages of food from home.

From Christmas until New Years I was still in bad shape from my cold and putting up with the nasty weather. New Years Eve some of the fellows had a party in one of the barracks but I went to bed and slept through it all. New Years day I relaxed and ate and slept, and by our next work day I was feeling better.

We had only about three weeks or so left of Basic. These last three weeks was going to be rough. The weather was starting to clear which was good because the big 20 mile, full field pack hike was coming up which was being cussed and discussed by everyone. We were to carry the full field pack with everything we owned plus metal helmets, rifles, bayonets, canteen, first-aid kit, and K-rations for one day. Altogether, this weighed almost one hundred pounds. We started out about 8:00 A.M. The first few miles were quite uneventful. We stopped for a break of about 10 minutes every hour.

At noon we took a lunch break eating our K-rations. The afternoon began quite well but after a few more miles, some of the men began to have problems. First one man, and then another, would fall out of formation to drag along behind. Some fell out completely. Finally, as we were beginning to feel as though each step might be our last, the camp began to come into view and with it the band. We got into step with the music and everything was okay, as we marched back to the parade ground to be dismissed. We then staggered back to our barracks, unpacked and fell on our bunks until we were called to fall out for chow. We staggered to our feet, fell out to formation and marched to the Mess Hall. We were hungry! We were tired but those of us who had completed the dreaded 20 mile hike somehow felt like soldiers now, not just recruits!

Our training now speeded up, more combat training, more shooting on the rifle range, with stationary targets and with moving targets. We had a contest on moving targets, in which I came out at 98%. For this I received an orderly, which meant that for one week I didn't have to polish my shoes or clean my rifle. The men with the poorest scores were the orderlies, who had to do the work for us for that one week. My 98% stood up as the best score in my whole barracks and was second best in the whole company.

Next came our training with pop up targets. We walked through a mock up town that had targets that would pop up to be shot at. We were scored by how many targets we hit and the location we hit the targets. We each had three times through the course to arrive at our average score. Each time through we became a little better at it. My average score was 94%. For this I received a 24 hour pass for the weekend. Several of us from our Company went together to Tyler for our 24 hour pass.

We were now down to our last week of Basic! We spent most of our last week out in the field, on bivouac. We slept in two-man pup tents, ate at the field kitchen, dug foxholes and let tanks run over us to simulate battle conditions. Saturday evening came and we packed up and marched back to camp and our barracks. Our showers sure felt good and so did our bunks. We rested and went to the PX Sunday afternoon for a couple of beers and some good music.

Monday morning we fell out to formation at 6:00 A.M. as usual, and we were told that we were no longer recruits, we were "soldiers." That same day they told us to pack and be all ready to move out. Every few hours there would be a call to formation, where they would call names of those to grab their packs and get ready to leave, then they handed out orders to those who were leaving so that they would know where to report. I had about two weeks before I was called, so I helped with the new recruits as they came in, to get them settled and learn the routine.

3

Part 3: Deployment: Fort Meade to Scotland

When my orders finally came I was to report to Fort Meade, Maryland after about a week's delay in route at home in Wisconsin. I rode the train from Kilgore to Chicago, then changed trains to take one to Portage by the Milwaukee Road. The time at home passed much too quickly, and I was soon back on the train headed for Ft. Meade. I felt very alone and lonely on that trip. I didn't know when I would see home again.

I arrived at Ft. Meade two days later, and there I met up with a few of the fellows that I had been in basic training with. We turned in all of our clothes the second day at Ft. Meade, and then we were issued all new clothes by the Army supply at Ft. Meade. We also received our overseas shots. One thing was the same as ever, it was fall out for roll-call at 6:00 A.M., back to the barracks to clean up, then fall out for formation to march to the Mess Hall. The food was really good and after chow, it was back to the barracks.

About 8:00 A.M. we fell out to formation to start the day. In the mornings we had calisthenics, or we went for five mile hikes, or got our shots, watched training films, and had lectures on Europe and what we could expect when we arrived there. We went back to the barracks about noon to clean up for chow. After chow it was back to the barracks to get ready for the afternoon. In my case, I was helping out in the supply room. With all the clothes being turned in and issuing new clothes to all of the men going overseas, it was a busy place.

We would work until 5:00 P.M. or so, then go back to the barracks, clean up and go to the Mess Hall. After chow we were free to go to Baltimore or Washington DC, which we usually did two nights a week. Both cities were close by with good bus service. The last bus back to Fort Meade was about 12:30 A.M., which gave us about an hour to sleep in our seats or above on the luggage rack back to the Fort. This would get us back into our bunks about 2:00 A.M. Our wake-up call came about 5:30 for 6:00 A.M. formation. This was the reason that we could only do that a couple of times a week.

We only spent about two and a half weeks at Ft. Meade before we were informed that we were shipping out to Camp Shanks, New York, which was a staging area for getting on board a ship to Europe. Camp Shanks was only a place where the Army could get all of the paperwork together for shipment overseas. We were only there four or five days. We then boarded a ferryboat setting sail down the Hudson River to board our ship. The Ile de France was the ship we boarded in New York harbor that night. This ship had been a luxury liner, being fast enough to make the Atlantic crossing by itself. The slower ships sailed in convoys so that the destroyer escorts could protect them from the German subs. We sailed the next day, which was about the third week in March, and were eight days aboard ship. We went on a zigzag course so that the German U-boats couldn't get a fix on our course. We also had complete blackout of the ship at night. There were small lights in the companionways and rooms below decks but none that would be visible from another ship or sub.

There were 800 WAC's and over 3200 men aboard our ship. This was a completely new experience for most of us. The crews were English and French. The cooks were English and were really busy even though we only had two meals per day. All areas were scheduled so that we could get fed, then move out of the way for the next group. To assure this, we were all issued passes with letters and numbers corresponding to the deck that we were on and the section number. I was on "E" deck, pretty far down in the hold. Our bunks were metal frames with canvas lashed to the frames with rope. Each set of bunks were four high and luckily I had the second bunk up from the deck. During the daytime we could go up on deck or walk around on the Promenade deck.

The second day out we got into the Gulf current that is always warm. The temperature warmed up into the low 70's. Two more days out, as we proceeded northeast, we were cold whenever on deck, even with our jackets on. We had been having emergency drills, but now we were being informed of the life expectancy in the water of the North Atlantic. These waters were so frigid, we were told, that five to six minutes were as long as you would likely live if we were torpedoed. All of this information really made us nervous for the rest of the trip. The seventh day out we passed to the north of the Irish coast. Of course everyone wanted to see land but the ship started to list precariously to port and we were quickly ordered to move to the starboard side.

Soon we were out of the sight of Ireland, sailing on to our destination in the Firth of Clyde near Glasgow, Scotland. We arrived on the eighth day out from New York. We were all relieved to be on solid ground again when they finally got us to shore. We were loaded on trucks and driven to a barracks just outside Glasgow. We were told to make ourselves at home but not to unpack. We ate in a large Mess Hall that afternoon, then were marched to a huge theater where they had a USO troupe to entertain us. We enjoyed it all immensely, except for some of the Scottish bagpipe music, but we gave them a huge round of applause anyway. We arrived back at our barracks about 8:30 or 9:00 P.M. and couldn't get to our bunks fast enough!

4

Part 4: Arrival in England and Joining the 1st Infantry Division

Morning came very early and at exactly 5:30 A.M., we were rudely awakened to stand formation, then marched over to the Mess Hall for breakfast in order to get ready to move again. This time they trucked us to a waiting train that would carry us south through the beautiful green countryside from Glasgow to England. This trip took us just a little over 24 hours. Quite often we were moved onto a sidetrack, while another train sped through. None of us could get over the green, green countryside.

  We arrived in Yeovil, England in late morning, where we were met by trucks to take us to an old English Army post situated about 2 miles outside Yeovil, a small town of about 12,000 people. The barracks were Quonset huts, where the bunks were made of a wooden frame three bunks high, with chicken wire nailed to them to hold mattress covers filled with straw. They weren't too bad, especially when we were tired. We spent a couple of days getting used to our new surroundings. Then there was a new element too, air raids from German bombers going over to bomb Bristol, England, which was a short distance north of our location. Every time the planes went over, we had to get out of the barracks and into the zigzag trenches dug around the barracks for that purpose.

About three days after I arrived, which was early in April, I was assigned to fireguard duty. This duty was okay because we had special passes at the Mess Hall to eat anytime that we wanted to. We also had special passes and seats at the movie theater, which was free to all of us on fireguard duty. We were on duty for 24 hours, on call or standby for 24 hours, and then off duty for 24 hours. During off duty times we were allowed to go to town or anywhere within 50 miles of camp. While on duty, we had to be in our barracks, at the Mess Hall, or in the fire station, nowhere else!

During my first 24 hours on duty there was an air raid alert. Those of us on fire guard duty were never allowed to get in the air raid trenches. We had to stand by our equipment in case there was a fire. The all clear signal sounded, so we went back to bed. Soon the air raid siren sounded again because the bombers were returning from Bristol, and this time the bombers dropped two bombs, as they sometimes did. When I heard the bombs screaming to earth I was sure that they were going to land right next to us but they landed about one mile away. Even at that distance it shook me up. That was the closest that any of the bombs landed during the rest of my fireguard duty.

When we were on standby duty we sometimes took one of our trailer pumps to town to practice while we filled the huge open tanks used by Yeovil as a back up water supplies for fires. We pulled our trailer pump with a jeep. I soon learned how to roll out hoses, to attach nozzles, and start the pump to pumping by watching the pressure gauges while turning the correct valves in sequence. It was while we were on the way back to camp one day from Yeovil, that we were forced off the road and into a ditch, causing me to be thrown out of the jeep, to land on all fours in a field. Of course I didn't stay on all fours after I hit the ground. I skidded on my belly, knees, and chin. I was able to get up and walk after a few minutes, but I was sore for a week.

A few days later I was off fireguard duty and back to the old barracks. They were preparing us to ship out to join regular Army outfits as replacements, to build up their strength before the invasion of Europe that was getting close now. We knew that we were all going to be involved in one way or the other. We now started to have full equipment formations. This meant that we had to stay packed up at all times, every time that we were asked to fall out, except for chow, we had to have all of our packs packed ready to move immediately. Every time that we fell out in full field packs, they would call out names and those men left immediately.

About four or five days later, on about the 5th or 6th of May, my name was called along with several other men. We marched out to trucks waiting for us and were driven to a spot near Weymouth, which is near the south coast of England.

There we joined the 1st Infantry Division, "The Big Red One!" I ended up with "I" Company of the 18th Infantry Regiment. The 1st Division has a fighting history during W.W.I and in North Africa and Sicily during W.W.II. Now we were getting ready for the invasion of Europe, and we knew that it was getting close, but we didn't know where or when just yet. Everyone was talking about the invasion and rumors were running rampant.

We new members started receiving our equipment, rifles, ammunition, and gas masks in special waterproof bags, known as assault masks. We also received new OD uniforms that were impregnated to guard against gas getting through to our skin. Of course, this meant going through the gas check chamber again to check the fit of our gas mask equipment, and to get them properly adjusted. We also had to go to the rifle range to check out our new rifles.

Our platoon leader was a 1st Lieutenant from Chicago who was a little squirrely. He was afraid of gas, so any time that we had a few spare moments, he would give us a lecture on taking care of our gas masks, then he would go into a lengthy lecture on the different types of gas and their reactions on the body. We started calling him "Lieutenant Gas," behind his back of course!

There were seventeen men in my squad, which was about five men over strength for the coming Invasion. The squad leader was T/Sgt. Joiner from Virginia, and the second in command of the squad was Sgt. Carl Dunn from southern Illinois. There was a 1st scout, 2nd scout, a three man B.A.R. Team (Browning Automatic Rifle), and the rest of us were riflemen.

The day that we went to the "rifle range" was the day that I met Daniel Ducey and MacGruer. Both of them were battle hardened men, having been with the 1st Division through battles in North Africa and Sicily. These two men were from another squad, but we got to talking and became friends. Daniel Ducey was a B.A.R. man, MacGruer was a rifleman and a real character. We were getting ready to fire our weapons.

The Company Commander, a "Captain" was giving the firing orders. It goes like this; "ready on the right, ready on the left, fire." At this point we were to fire one shot at a time until the order comes to stop firing. On the order to fire, MacGruer fired his whole clip of ammo. The Captain hollered, "hold your fire" then, "who fired that shot?" MacGruer spoke up, "Captain, that was a whole clip!" The Captain ordered him to "dry fire" the rest of the day, no ammo for MacGruer. Ducey, MacGruer, and I were to cross paths many times after that.

5

Part 5: D-Day: The Omaha Beach Landing and Advance Inland

We received word to get ready to move out into marshaling areas to get ready for the coming INVASION. Again we had to be in a state of readiness. This meant packing up and staying packed at all times!

After we moved into the marshaling area, we lived as though on bivouac, and started to receive lectures on the part that we would play in the invasion of Europe. The 1st Division would lead the assault on Omaha Beach on the north coast of France and spearhead the attack into France. We also began practicing climbing up and down rope ladders with all of our equipment. Our equipment for this was field packs, rifles, assault gas masks, ammo including grenades, and now we wore life belts that we wore up under our arms. These could be inflated by pulling a little ring. These were to be inflated only in case we dropped into deep water from our L.C.A. craft.

We (the 18th Regimental Combat Team) were scheduled to land on (Easy Red-Omaha Beach) beginning at 9:30 A.M. This was to be the THIRD WAVE. The first landings (FIRST WAVE) that morning were to be at 6:30 A.M. by the 16th Regimental Combat Team along with the 116th Regimental Combat Team. The 115th Infantry attached from the

29th Division, and the Provisional Ranger Force made up of the 2nd and 5th Battalions of Rangers, made up what was to be known as Force "O". Total men numbered 34,142 with 3,306 vehicles.

During the last few days of May, we started moving again toward the Portland Harbor for the purpose of loading onto ships. Sometime during this movement there was an enemy air attack on the Weymouth area which was fairly close by, but we only lost a few small crafts and sustained only a few casualties.

We finally boarded ship and the waiting began. The weather was bad, rain and wind. The afternoon of June 5th, we started moving out of Portland Harbor. The weather was still nasty, the English Channel is always rough but this was worse than normal with most of the men getting sick. I came very close to being sick, but managed to keep everything down. We were in cramped quarters with nowhere to put our equipment but on our bunks, berths or whatever they were called. We hardly slept at all that night and no one talked much. Each man had his own private thoughts about what would happen the next day. D-DAY was only a few hours away.

We were all up early on June 6th, the cooks had to get us all fed a hot meal so that we would be ready to go. The food was brought to our area, I was hungry but couldn't eat very much. Not too many of the men ate much because of a combination of nerves and the fact that the ship was pitching and rolling from four to five foot waves. The winds were still blowing hard but it was slowly clearing. The rain had stopped and visibility was about 10 miles as the morning mist over the channel cleared. By the time that we got on deck all that we could see, no matter which direction we looked, was ships, ships and more ships of all types and descriptions.

Then all of a sudden, there was a terrific barrage of gunfire from Navy ships, firing toward the shore of France. Bombers appeared in the sky, through the partial overcast, also heading for the shore to help in the bombardment of the German positions on the coast of France. Sunrise was at 5:58 A.M. that morning with the 1st wave scheduled at 6:30 A.M. to hit the beach at low tide. We knew that this bombardment was for our benefit but it was still an awful shock to us to hear so much noise from the shells and bombs on shore. Just imagine what it must have sounded like to the enemy on shore. Soon the noise let up as the shells landed farther inland and the bombers bombed farther inland, for it was time for the 1st wave to hit the beach.

    Soon it was time for us to load onto our L.C.A.'s (Landing Craft Assault) that would carry us into that beach. We lined up, went over the side onto rope ladders that were wide enough for four of us to climb down side by side to the waiting L.C.A., which was bobbing up and down at least four or five feet, sometimes more. Some of the men jumped as the L.C.A. was going down, which made them land hard while others were left dangling from the rope ladder. I was lucky, only falling about 2 feet. As soon as we were aboard the L.C.A., we helped the others land until we were all loaded.

    Our L.C.A. then proceeded to go in a large easy circle pattern until all were ready to head for the beach. We were still about two miles from the Beach when we began to run into traffic. There was absolute chaos in the water with craft of all descriptions maneuvering in every direction. Because of all the congestion, we could not steer a straight course or stay in any type of formation toward the beach. We were scheduled to land at 9:30 A.M., but it became impossible to keep that deadline.

    By the time that we were a mile or so out, we had to cut our speed even more and to constantly veer away from floating debris, bodies and half submerged vehicles. We finally reached the beach about 10:00 A.M. or shortly thereafter. We were lucky in one respect, because our landing craft made its way through the litter in the water's edge, so when the ramp lowered we stepped out into only about two feet of water.

    What a sight greeted us as we waded onto the beach; bodies floating in the water, bodies lying all over the beach, tractors, tanks, vehicles, bulldozers, and men running in all directions. It was utter and complete chaos with shells landing in amongst us and small arms fire coming from the bluff above us.

There were also mines on the beach with only some sections cleared. These sections had been marked with ribbons but these ribbons had been ripped away by shells, etc., only to blow in the strong wind.

We started across the beach toward the shingle in what we thought might be a cleared section, but when we were almost to the shingle (the section right under or next to the bluff wall) one of our squad members stepped on a mine that exploded. We looked back in time to see a body being blown apart, and two other men nearby at the tail end of the squad were wounded.

Once we got to the shingle, we moved along it to our left but were told to hold up, because there was an enemy pillbox on top of the bluff overlooking the entrance to E-1 draw. A tank on the beach had tried to fire on it without success. Under the direction of a naval observer on the beach with us, a destroyer opened fire on the pillbox. After a few rounds to zero in, the destroyer hit the pillbox right in the opening, knocking it out of commission.

Now the engineers, with covering fire from us, were able to go up the draw a ways, then up onto the bluff. We had to fight all of the way, but we finally reached the top of the bluff. Someone remarked that "Easy Red" wasn't easy, but it sure was red from all the blood spilled there!

We were still being shot at by the enemy, so it still was not any picnic after we reached the top of the bluff, but we were all happy to be off that beach! We reached the high ground just beyond the bluff by shortly after noon. The enemy resistance was very stiff in this area as we moved south from the bluffs, there were small bands or pockets of the enemy behind us as well as in front of us, but we didn't have time to clean them out so we just kept going, leaving the pockets to be cleaned out by other troops coming on behind us.

By late afternoon our ammo was getting in short supply. Our artillery and tanks were almost non-existent at this point, because so much of it had been swamped on the way into the beach or had been destroyed on the beach itself. The enemy artillery, however, had moved to the south and set up new positions to fire into us, and onto the beach.

Our mission was to keep moving south, to our objectives near Colleville. We were soon issued alternate plans to take over the mission and objectives of the 16th Regiment. We now started to move to the south and east of Colleville through the evening twilight. Sunset that day was at 10:10 P.M. so it was still partly light until about 11:00 P.M. We kept moving through the night and into the morning of June 7th.

The Germans were slowly retreating to a place where they could dig in to hold their ground but we kept running into pockets of resistance. By shortly after noon we were in Surrain, reaching the Bayeux highway around 5:00 P.M.

We crossed the Aure River that evening, arriving at a stopping point where we could dig in southeast of Mandeville shortly after midnight. We still had to dig in which took us a couple of hours. By early morning on June 8th we had been on the move for 72 hours with no hot food, only our D-ration bars and water.

We did receive some ammo and grenades, then we were attacked by the enemy shortly after dawn, which engaged us in a fierce firefight. It was a good thing that we had dug in as well as we had or we could have lost a lot of men that morning. The 2nd Division came to relieve us so that we could assemble the whole 18th Regiment southwest of Mosles on high ground. Because of the firefight that we were engaged in, it was difficult for our relief to take over our positions. We were finally able to withdraw but had to march a considerable distance to reach our assembly area.

We finally reached our assembly area where we received more ammo, ate a hot meal, then we set out on our new mission. This time we had tanks and field artillery in support. We also had 6 inch guns from the Navy cruisers that could be called in when needed. The Navy had sent along Navy observers to call in fire from the cruisers.

Our 18th Regiment, with the 26th Regiment on our left, moved out on a 4000 yard front. The 16th Regiment was behind us, in reserve. We moved slowly fighting against stubborn resistance all day. By 9:00 P.M. we were two miles behind the 26th, so the 16th was brought up to guard the 26th flank, but by daylight we had pulled up even with the 26th again and both were nearing the objectives set out for us. By late afternoon of June 10th, we had taken our objectives on the edge of Carisy Forest.

On June 11th, the whole 1st Division began organizing the ground taken in our rapid advance. This meant cleaning out the remaining enemy pockets and the snipers hidden behind during our advance. The ground needed for the security of the beachhead had been won and secured. We had moved over 12 miles inland at this particular point in time. We now learned that the principal objective in the next phase was the Caumont area. Caumont lies on a hilly area more than 750 feet above sea level controlling the upper Drome Valley. Its capture would make the hold on the beachhead doubly secure.

Again the 18th, with the 26th on the left, would be side by side, each on fronts of about 3000 yards, with the 16th in reserve. The jump off was scheduled for 6:00 A.M. June 12th. Again we met only slight resistance from small groups of the enemy. By evening we had made a four mile advance to the Caumont-St. Lo highway.

We were halted there, but told to patrol the area ahead and to our right flank. The 26th had pulled to the edge of Caumont, but their patrols found Caumont held by the Germans. With first light on June 13th, the 26th Regiment and elements of the 743rd Tank Battalion cleared the Village of Caumont in house to house fighting.

We spent June 13th in organizing our positions for all-around defense

PART 5: D-DAY: THE OMAHA BEACH LANDING AND ADVANCE INLAND

and in patrolling forward from our lines and to the flanks. By late afternoon, we were receiving attacks from enemy patrols. The German artillery was also being felt in Caumont, as well as the surrounding area. The 1st Division had moved forward so quickly that the 2nd Division on our right, and the British forces on our left, were behind us about two miles. The whole 1st Division was out on a limb and the enemy was trying their best to cut the limb off. We dug in, making our positions and defenses as good as possible.

From June 13th until July 14th, we held those positions. We waited for the enemy to counter-attack, going on night patrols into the enemy territory and probing the enemy line of defenses. At night, we put outposts of four or five men out in front of our lines every 20 yards or so. Outpost duty was very scary, watching for the enemy to try to sneak in on us. During this time we were shelled by the enemy artillery almost every day. On July 14th, the 5th Division relieved us so that we could go to a bivouac area where we would rest and re-equip for a new offensive push.

We marched to the rear and in a swinging arc ended up to the northwest in our bivouac area near the little Norman village of Colombiars. Here, we did rest and re-equip. It was here that I made a huge mistake by calling the Lieutenant, Lt. Gas to his face. I knew better, but it just slipped out! He sent me to the company Mess Sgt. to do KP Duty. I helped dig the sump hole for the company kitchen, but also got acquainted with the Mess Sgt. who was a nice fellow. He liked the fact that I appreciated good coffee, so I ended up making the coffee for the company for the next few days, and never did pull KP duty. We got into an all night black-jack game that night and I ended up winning a little over $75.00. This was big bucks when you are making $50.00 to $60.00 a month, Army pay.

I also ran into Daniel Ducey and MacGruer. That same night MacGruer got drunk and knocked down Lieutenant Gas's tent. The Lieutenant was also drunk when he crawled out from under the tent on his hands and knees. MacGruer jumped on the Lieutenant's back to try his hand at bronc riding. Needless to say MacGruer was transferred to Company H.Q. the next day.

6

Part 6: Operation COBRA and the Fight for Marigny

As we had figured, we weren't to be in rest very long. The 1st Division was transferred from V Corp. to VII Corp. The 1st Division was ordered to Coil itself tight behind the 9th, 4th, and 30th Divisions for operation "COBRA". On July 19th the 1st Division moved into the assembly area behind the 9th Division. We remained there waiting for the weather to clear for air support. July 25th dawned clear, this was just the type of weather needed for the bombers to do the saturation bombing in the area ahead of the Assault Infantry Divisions. The sky was full of bombers (1500 heavy bombers, then medium bombers and finally small fighter bombers came in low to finish the job). The ground shook from all the bombs dropping near St. Lo, even though we were about four miles away at the time. The smoke from the first bombs drifted back over the 9th Division, the following bombers bombed two Battalions of the 9th Division, nearly wiping them out. Naturally, the 1st Division was called on to pass through the 9th Division, to attack while the enemy was still in a state of shock from the bombing. We fought our way into the little village of Marigny on July 26th. During this time we lost our 1st Scout, who was either killed or captured. I was called on to be 1st Scout for our

Squad. This was not my idea of a good position, because I was now being set up to be shot or captured.

We didn't make much headway that night. The next morning July 27th, we started past the little catholic church and on into the village of Marigny. There was fierce fighting through the little village, but finally we were beyond it.

While crossing a field at the edge of town, an enemy machine-gun opened fire on us. For some reason, I remembered my training, looking for any depression I could find before I hit the ground running. We called in for artillery support which cleared the area ahead of us quite well.

When the firefight was over, the whole B.A.R. team behind me were all dead, all three men. The squad leader then picked another man to be 1st Scout. I became the B.A.R. team. We were getting short of men in our squad, actually in the whole company, so I did not have any help carrying that heavy B.A.R., which I ended up carrying for some time.

There was an important crossroads to be taken near Marigny so we battled with the enemy the rest of the day and into the evening. This crossroads was important to the Germans as well as it was to us. They did not intend to give it up without a fight. During probing patrols near Marigny, a gap was found in the enemy line of about 300 yards. Combat team 16 was set up to go through the gap. It was a huge gamble, but with prompt action and speed, the 16th made their way through the gap during the night of July 27th, with other units following to widen the gap and to help encircle the Germans.

During this time we moved, fought firefights, moved, fought firefights again, until time no longer registered with us. It was either light or it was dark, but the time or day of the week or month never mattered as long as we were able to meet our objective time table. Our planes were out in force, hitting railroads and convoys of troop, so that reserve forces couldn't be brought in. Our planes also hit armored columns of Germans trying to move back from our onslaught.

During this time, about July 29th or 30th, we crossed the Soulle River somewhere near Coutances. I was ordered to set up my B.A.R., along with 2 other men from other squads with B.A.R.'s, three machine guns, two tanks, and two bazookas. We were to fire our weapons for support while the rest of our Company crossed the river to attack a German stronghold in a big French Chateau, on a hill above the river. Daniel Ducey was one of the other B.A.R. men. We continued to provide support fire until we ran short on ammo. The barrels of our B.A.R.'s got so hot that we burned our hands while trying to hold them down.

Daniel Ducey went over to the tanks to borrow ammo for us and a man to load our clips, so that we could keep firing. In the early afternoon, we were ordered to join our Company up on the hill. We moved across the river, through a wooded area, where we found a narrow road that let through the woods and up the hill to the chateau. Our men were all past the chateau, where they were covering the hill.

As we were walking past the chateau, something caught my eye in the window. I turned firing my B.A.R. at the window. Two of the enemy fell out through the window. A firefight started then, and all we could do was stand and return fire into the chateau. Daniel Ducey was hit and died a few minutes later.

The rest of us headed for the door of the chateau, but the Germans that were still alive decided to surrender. We took all of the prisoners, about eight, to start them back down through the woods to the river. About this time the rest of our Company came back, because a German tank with about fifteen to eighteen men arrived. We all retreated back to the river.

At the river, the other men with machine guns and us two with our B.A.R.'s, covered the rest of our Company as they retreated across the river. Soon another Company of men arrived, and along with our Company and several tanks, we went back up through the wooded area to take the high ground again near the chateau. By early evening we were dug in on high ground.

That night I got to thinking about some of the men I had been friends with, who were now dead. You can't help being close to those you fight with, you see each other at your very worst, but somehow I knew that I couldn't let myself get really close to these men. It hurts too much to see them die.

That evening MacGruer came by, he had been out on a patrol into a little village to the southeast of our position. Part of "I" Company, and two other Companies, were in house to house combat there. MacGruer had a bullet hole through his canteen, his pant legs had burn marks and holes from bullets. He sat talking for quite awhile about Ducey and what a sad thing war was. That was the last time I saw MacGruer until September.

7

Part 7: The Breakout and the Argentan-Falaise Pocket

The next morning we jumped off early, heading for the Sienne River in the Gavray area. Our planes were out in force during the daylight hours, hitting some very good targets in the enemy areas and along the roads.

At night the Germans brought out their bombers, and we could always tell it was them, because they had a very funny sound to their engines. This night, July 31st, the JU-88 bombers droned overhead dropping flares, then proceeded to bomb all our positions as well as 1st Division Headquarters. This even disrupted our communications for over half an hour or so. They also dropped anti-personnel bombs with delayed action fuses throughout the whole area. These bombs kept exploding long after the bombers had left the area. This was the worst bombing that I experienced during the whole war.

The following morning found us licking our wounds and jumping off again to cross the Sienne River. We kept moving southeast until we arrived near Mortain. On or about August 5th, we were relieved by the 30th Division. Our whole Division moved out onto rural roads to start the move to Mayenne. It was a very difficult march because we had been fighting night and day for so long, with very little sleep. The only good thing was that the sound of artillery barrages and small arms' fire was far in the distance now.

Ahead of us, Combat Team 16 hit the village of Mayanne, taking the town. We just followed along behind, tired but happy not to be in the fight. We now started marching in a huge arc that brought us around to head northeast, then finally north toward Couterne. During this time an artillery (Cub) spotter plane flying low, spotted some German trucks half camouflaged under some trees, near Aron. Artillery was called on. They hit the trucks and half-tracks, flushing out German troops, tanks, and artillery, etc. Dive bombers were called on to help by bombing the whole column of the enemy in that area.

German troops and armor were still trying to escape from the beach area. The huge pincer movement that we were closing had trapped the whole Seventh German Army, with only remnants of the SS Panzer Divisions escaping. Thus, on or about August 19th, the Argentan-Falaise pocket was almost closed with the artillery and Army Air Corp pounding the ever shrinking pocket. The roads and hill sides down through that valley were littered with thousands of the enemy dead and wounded, wrecked and burning tanks, vehicles, smashed artillery, dead horses, and overturned carts.

We could see the fires at night from the hills along the southeast side of this area. This helped us because there was little further trouble except for isolated detachments of the enemy. Now sweat replaced blood as we marched on and on, only occasionally did we receive a ride for a few miles on a truck, half-track, or tank.

At long last we stopped marching. The whole 1st Division was again assembled in a bivouac area. We rested and re-armed, so we knew that we were getting ready for another big push. It was on my birthday, August 23rd, that we received orders to move out the next day. This time we did ride on trucks, because we moved about 96 miles that day, to Courville.

We only stayed overnight in a bivouac area, then moved out again on August 25th to push through Etamps, another 55, miles to our next assigned bivouac area. The next morning we jumped off early, marching again shortly after sunrise. We headed for the Seine River south of Paris arriving at the river about midday. We had to cross the river on a pontoon bridge because the original bridge had been bombed out.

We had just crossed the bridge when men began falling out to lie on the ground. Except for a very few days, we had been on the move, walking until we were all tired out. Several Companies fell out that day, so after about an hour of no movement, the "Brass" decided to put us on wheels!

Trucks, tanks, half-tracks, jeeps, and all sorts of vehicles were put into service to get us going again. From that point on, all the way into Belgium, we would move for 25 or 30 miles, running into small groups of Germans that had escaped form the Argentan-Falaise pocket. We would get off the vehicles, round up or kill the Germans, quite often it would erupt into a firefight, and sometimes they would surrender. The ones that surrendered were turned over to our MP's to guard, while taking them back to the cages built for them. These Germans were completely surprised by us because they were escaping across northern France with no clue to where we were. They were just trying to get back to Germany.

We kept moving northeast across France, and it was during this time that we ran into a fairly large group of Germans, about dusk. We got into a real firefight that lasted several hours. My squad was lying on the ground in whatever concealment we could find. The Germans started throwing grenades amongst us, some coming real close.

One grenade landed so close, that it picked me up off the ground almost a foot, and my left ear and my nose started to bleed from the concussion. I could hardly hear anything for several hours. We were finally able to beat them back with the help of the rest of our Company. We found out that we had been fighting a parachute company of Germans. We were happy to have it over with so that we could get to our assigned bivouac area for the night.

8

Part 8: Advance into Belgium and the Siegfried Line

We reached Soisson about August 31st. Soisson was the scene of fighting by the 1st Division during W.W.I. There was an International Cemetery there and a monument to the 1st Division telling of the roll they played during WW1. There was also this quote from General Pershing's tribute to his own 1st Division.

   THE COMMANDER-IN-CHIEF HAS NOTED IN THIS DIVISION A SPECIAL PRIDE IN SERVICE AND A HIGH STATE OF MORALE, NEVER BROKEN BY HARDSHIP OR BATTLE.

   We raced on toward Belgium and whatever lay ahead. At almost every crossroads we would run into small groups of Germans. It was becoming a problem with all of the prisoners that we were taking. We could only disarm them and hand them over to the MP's. There weren't enough MP's to take all of the prisoners back to the cages. Sometimes two MP's would escort a hundred prisoners or more. There were many strange stories to come out of this particular part of the war. Stories of enemy tanks joining with our tanks in the twilight hours. Enemy troops walking into our bivouac area at night not even knowing we were anywhere in the area.

PART 8: ADVANCE INTO BELGIUM AND THE SIEGFRIED LINE

One German tank pulled into our bivouac area with some of our tanks, but an alert MP noticed the markings on the side of the tank, alerting everyone. The German crew surrendered, then said they were almost out of gas. We were feeling the supply pinch too. Our supply lines were getting longer and we had been moving so fast that we were running low on ammo, gas for our vehicles, cigarettes, and food. We received orders to conserve supplies. How do you conserve ammo or gas when you are moving the way that we had been moving?

More than 17,000 prisoners were taken by the 1st Division alone during this time. We fought our way into the Mons, Belgium area, then spent five days fighting against remnants of the First German Army, who had also been cut off from returning to Germany by our rapid advance. On September 7th, we pulled out of Mons now heading southeast toward Charleroi. Our first night in Charleroi, we went on patrol in our assigned sector with three jeeps, which turned out to be pretty quiet.

Just as we returned to Company H.Q. to report in we ran into MacGruer who was now at the Company motor pool as a jeep driver. He invited Sgt. Carl Dunn and myself to go to Brussels the next day with him. Because we were to be in Charleroi for at least two or three days, we received permission to accompany MacGruer. Except for MacGruer's wild driving, this little trip was a pleasant change of pace for us. We returned that evening from Brussels in time to go on jeep patrol again. Except for some drunken American soldiers, the patrol was quiet.

The next day we received orders to move out again toward Liege, then on toward Eupen, finally we turned toward Aachen, Germany and the Siegfried Line. The Siegfried Line was a highly defended line of tank traps, pillboxes and booby trapped areas, built by the Germans to protect their own soil. We jumped off at 8:00 A.M. on September 12th toward the Siegfried Line. There was much resistance by the enemy now because they were protecting their own soil, the Fatherland.

We fought all day with hardly any headway. We were to capture all of the high ground south and southwest of Aachen. When we had taken that area, we were relieved by another outfit so that we could relieve the 26th Regiment in the Siegfried Line at or near Stolberg on September 14th or 15th. We fought our way through the Siegfried Line until September 21st. On the morning of September 22nd, we in the 3rd Battalion of the 18th Regiment were attached to the 16th Regiment to relieve the 83rd Armored Reconnaissance Battalion. We were in the Siegfried Line, so close to Stolberg (only about 2 miles away) that we could see it from the pillbox that our squad occupied.

On the night of September 23rd we were shelled by the German artillery with phosphorous shells. Phosphorous is bad because if it gets on your skin it will burn right through It also is used for marking positions because it gives off smoke when it lands. We now could look for an attack because they were zeroing in with the phosphorous shells! Early in the morning of September 24th, just about daylight, we pulled our outpost guards into the pillbox just before the shelling started. The enemy artillery laid down a very heavy barrage. Then they attacked us with small arms, mortars, machine guns, and bazookas, from about 6:00 A.M. until 1:00 P.M., when they all pulled back.

All of a sudden, we could hear a tank moving around outside very nearby. We thought to ourselves oh, no!, if this is a German tank, we are goners! We opened the two doors to the pillbox, and stepped out to see three of our tanks advancing down the road. One tank was also behind us ready to blow us up if we had been the enemy. Our whole Regiment had been hit hard that day. We sure were happy to see the tanks and supporting troops. We spent the next two days consolidating our positions before we were relieved on September 29th. We found out that we had been fighting an SS Battalion from three years on the Russian Front. During their fight with our Regiment the whole Battalion had been decimated.

9

Part 9: The Battle for Aachen and Hand-to-Hand Combat

I was now transferred from the 1st Squad to become 2nd in command of the 3rd Squad. This meant a promotion to Buck Sergeant, as we now moved once again several miles over muddy roads to a new area as part of the 1st Division surrounding of Aachen. The weather had started to get nasty. It rained a lot over the next several days while we were moving into a new attack towards Haaren.

Around 7:30 A.M. on October 10th we launched an attack on Haaren, taking the area by 10:35 A.M., then doing mop up operations through October 11th. Near Haaren was some high ground called Crucifix Hill that the 2nd Battalion, as well as our 3rd Battalion, was fighting to take from the enemy. We managed to take part of the high ground but the Germans threw everything at us in a giant counter attack, but we were able to hold on. Along with our artillery, we finally were able to disperse them enough to continue our attack on through the evening and through the night. By morning we were able to take all of the high ground and establish road blocks on the Weiden-Aachen road. We then jumped off toward Ravelsberg near Aachen.

Our supply lines were long but the Germans were now close to their supplies and supply dumps. Our food supply was also short now. We captured a German supply dump, so we started eating sauerkraut and polish sausage along with our own food. At this point I started to hate the damn Germans and their food. Cigarettes were short, coffee was short and our tempers were becoming short. Every foot of land that we took had to be fought for now. The rain not only bothered us, but the tanks got bogged down and the planes couldn't fly air support for us. We were near Aachen now, fighting in the mud and rain to take our objective, which was Ravelsberg.

At 2:30 P.M. on October 19th the enemy launched a new attack at us in Ravelsberg, supported by tanks, and self propelled guns. During the next two and one half hours we did push the enemy back some, but sustained many casualties in heavy hand-to-hand fighting. This was my first and only hand-to-hand combat. I can only say that it was ugly! In most combat situations it is very impersonal, but in hand-to-hand combat everything becomes very personal because you are toe to toe and eye to eye. I was pretty badly beaten up but I did survive the whole experience, so I think that I was very lucky! I was pulled out that afternoon and sent to the hospital in Liege. I was sick and running a fever for several days, so I don't remember too much that happened.

10

Part 10: Wounded, AWOL in Paris, and Court Martial

We arrived at the Hospital in Liege, Belgium sometime toward morning on October 21st. I was not sure what was happening. At the hospital in Liege, my temperature was brought down but I was sedated because I was in pain. I do know that I was moved by ambulance to a waiting train that took a large group of us back through Paris and on to a tent hospital near Carentan, France that was not far from Utah Beach.

   I spent several days at this tent hospital resting, having some dental work done, while they gave me antibiotics to clear up my injuries. I had seven teeth drilled and filled in one sitting with the dentist using an old foot operated drill. I believe that this is why I came to hate seeing a dentist. After a few days of rest, good food, and the antibiotics I began to feel better. Everyone was talking about a Halloween party at the hospital. One of the nurses that I became acquainted with asked me to attend the Halloween party with her, and of course I agreed to go. The party turned out great, and everyone had a good time.

   Three days later I received orders that I was being released from the hospital to return to the Front. It seems as though some of the doctors were very upset that five of us enlisted men went to the party with nurses (who were officers). Every one of us five received orders to ship out immediately. Coincidence? I don't think so!

On November 7th, we boarded a train at Carentan. This turned out to be a freight train and we were loaded into 40 and 8 box cars. The term 40 and 8, is from WW1, when those same cars would carry 40 men or 8 horses. There were 47 of us men in the car that I rode in. What a crowded situation that was. We had to change off sitting on the floor or standing because there wasn't room for all of us to sit at once. We rode all day in this fashion.

The train moved very slowly then would pull onto a siding (side-tracks) quite often to let trainloads of supplies go by. We didn't have a very high priority. In the late afternoon of that first day our train pulled onto a siding where they had army trucks with food waiting for us. What a pleasant surprise it was to see the hot food and coffee. After eating we all crawled back on the train, ready to move again. That night was bad, we traded positions about every two hours, standing, then sitting, then standing again. By morning everyone was complaining. About mid-morning we pulled onto a siding where our breakfast was waiting for us. Hot coffee and pancakes sure tasted good. After eating, we climbed back aboard our 40 and 8 cars again, but this time our car wasn't quite as crowded, because we had lost a few men. By early afternoon we were complaining again because there still wasn't room to all sit down at once. We pulled onto a siding to wait for another train to go by.

Four of us got out of our car and crawled behind some old bombed out buildings. We waited for about an hour after our train pulled out, then headed for a nearby road. Once on the road we hitched a ride on a truck carrying supplies, for this was the Red Ball Highway that carried supplies to the Front.

This truck was much more comfortable than standing up half of the time on the train. The truck driver stopped in a little village along the way for some French bread and a couple of bottles of wine. The bread and wine lasted until late afternoon when the driver pulled into an Army Railroad Company where he was acquainted. We were all fed a good meal before climbing back into the truck to continue our journey. We were heading for Paris but our driver was heading northeast toward Belgium so we parted at Dreax, France.

We once again started hitchhiking a ride. We received a short ride of fifteen to twenty miles. This brought us almost to the outskirts of Paris. We found a room for the night where all four of us could stay together. We found a Boulangerie close by for some French bread and a small cafe for a couple of bottles of wine to wash it down.

Next morning we were out early trying to hitch a ride but ran into a couple of MP's. We of course didn't have passes or anything except our story that the train ran off leaving us to fend for ourselves. The MP's took us to their headquarters near Le Mons while they checked us out. Our story didn't sound too far fetched so after a few hours they took us to a holding area where there were about twenty-five other men.

We finally were fed in the late afternoon, then put on board Army trucks with canvas tops over the backs. It was starting to rain and very chilly, even with the canvas tops. We were driven to a guarded camp area, given blankets then escorted to pup tents, where we were to sleep. It rained hard all night, and we didn't sleep very well.

When morning came it was still raining but we rolled out as ordered to stand in line in the rain for our breakfast. At least they had a big tent set up for a mess hall so that we could eat under cover. After breakfast we went back to our tents. Now that it was daylight we could see that we were in a barbed wire enclosure with high observation posts on every corner, with two guards with machine guns. This looked more like a POW camp.

We stayed at this detention camp for two days and it rained hard every day that we were there. The third day at this camp, some of us were lined up and marched out to two waiting trucks. We were driven to a replacement depot in a huge French chateau near Paris. At the replacement depot things were even worse.

We did have cots to sleep on but no mess kits or utensils with which to eat our meals. When we asked about eating utensils we were told to borrow what we needed. We did try borrowing utensils, but by the time that we got into the chow line, almost everything was gone. Several of us who had been at the detention camp got our heads together to decide what to do next. We decided that it would have to be one of two things, steal eating utensils or walk away again.

We took a vote and decided that we would walk away in groups of two or three. Another fellow whom we called Boston and I (I was Frenchie) teamed up to go together. We left late that afternoon heading for Paris.

This time Boston and I were lucky, making it all of the way into Paris. Boston spoke some French, enough to be able to ask directions, etc. On November 16th, which was my mother's birthday, we arrived in Paris. Boston asked directions to take the Metro to the Montmarte District of Paris.

We arrived in the Montmarte District after a few minor problems. We walked around the area checking it out, while watching for MP's. Paris was really something, even during this particular time. The city had only recently become free after several years of German occupation. There were several small night clubs in this area of Paris.

We ran into a fellow from New Orleans who ran a small night club in Montmarte. Maurice was his name and he was very nice to us, even furnishing us with a room. One evening while drinking more than usual, he told us that he was a deserter from the U. S. Army. He had sold a truck load of gasoline that he had been driving, truck and all. He had sold it to people in the French black-market.

He then led the MP's to where the black-market people had hidden it and several other truck loads. Maurice then deserted with the money for which he had sold his truck and load. After checking around, Maurice bought this night club from the Frenchman that owned it. This was only one of many stories that we heard during the few days and nights that we spent in Paris.

Paris was fun but expensive, and anytime that we were on the street we had to be constantly on the alert for MP's or O.S.S. agents. Cigarettes cost a dollar a pack on the black-market, and food was also expensive. We worked out a little deal with Maurice to bring U.S. soldiers into the night club to help pay for our cigarettes and food.

About six days after we arrived in Paris, we were finally picked up by the MP's. It was evening, we had already had a few drinks and we were not alert enough to notice them. We were taken to a detention hall where there were dozens of G.I.'s. We were clean, but many of the G.I.'s had their pockets and the inside of their jackets full of candy, gum, cigarettes, etc., which they had been selling to the black-market people. Now they were trying to get rid of everything.

They offered to give us cartons of cigarettes, candy, gum, whatever, just so they wouldn't get caught with all those things. We were in the detention hall most of the night because the MP's only took three men at a time into the interrogation room where there were three tables set up. At the table we had to empty our pockets, then we were searched completely, then the interrogation began.

After the question and answer session, all of our possessions were put into a bag, labeled, and we were sent to another room to wait. When they had eighteen men in this waiting room, they were loaded into a truck and driven to the old French prison on the edge of Paris. Here we were herded into a large holding cell, called the "tank". It was probably 12:30 to 1:00 A.M. by the time that we were put in the "tank". It was cold, with a cement floor, and no place to sit except on the floor. There must have been sixty of us in one big room.

At this point Boston and I were still together. We all tried to stand close together for body heat, and it worked to a certain extent but the body odor was terrific. About 4:00 A.M. someone found a cigarette lighter that hadn't been confiscated, so someone got the bright idea of standing on each other's shoulders to get at the wood trim that was about ten feet up the wall all around the room. When we had the trim all pulled down from the walls, it was broken up and set afire.

The idea hadn't been thought through very well, however, because there was no place for the smoke to get out of the room! By the time that the MP's came in to put out the fire, we were all very black and smoky but warmer. The MP's soon took us out of the "tank" and marched us to our cells. It was a little warmer there and we had bunks to lie down on for a few hours.

Around 8:00 A.M. we were marched to our breakfast. This was a whole new experience too, as we went through a line to receive our food, then to tables that were chest high. We didn't sit down to eat but moved slowly along the table eating as we moved, and when we reached the end of the table we were through eating, no matter what! I lucked out again, I only spent one day here. The second day I was moved along with about thirty other men to another holding camp where we received our Summary Court Martial.

All thirty of us were needed back at the Front, so it was a hurry up affair to get us Court Martialed and on our way back to the Front. I was brought up before a Major for my Summary Court Martial proceedings. He read the charges against me, being AWOL, etc., then he started to lecture me about my dereliction of duty, etc. He also told me about his entering France on D+10 or 11 and how it was.

I listened to him politely, then said "Sir, I landed on Easy Red, Omaha Beach on D-day, H-hour +4. I doubt very much if you could understand how it was unless you were there at that time. Anyway, you can't tell me much about Omaha Beach that I don't know from first hand experience. I also spent over four months at the Front fighting with the 1st Infantry Division. I could tell you things that would curl your hair. We weren't brave, we were afraid, afraid not to do our best against whatever odds we might be up against. That was what our training was all about. Also, it taught us not to take unnecessary chances while doing a necessary, nasty job. What we had to do in battle, that was about dying! What I have just been doing is about living! I expect that now I will go back to the 1st Division to fight for however long I might live! If I do live, I will have won."

The Major just looked at me for a few minutes, finally he said, "Sgt. French, you are no longer a Sgt. Your rank is Private, you are being fined $100.00 and you will spend seven days at hard labor which may be suspended so that you can return to your Division immediately. You are dismissed." That is all there was to it, so I returned to the waiting room as one by one each of the men received their Court Martial.

We broke for lunch and we were marched to the Mess Hall. After lunch we went to our rooms for about half an hour. About 1:00 P.M., we were all marched back to the waiting room for the rest of the afternoon while the Officers finished with the rest of the men. Everything moved along fairly fast so that by 4:30 P.M. or so all of us thirty men had been court martialed. We were marched to the Mess Hall again, fed, and returned to our rooms to collect our things and get ready to move out.

We were then loaded on to trucks to begin another journey, where to, we didn't know. As the night passed into dawn it became increasingly clear to us that this was going to be a long trip. When it became light enough to see clearly, we could make out the names of the villages, and see we were getting close to Belgium. We stopped to eat about 8:00 A.M. at an Army MP base in Belgium, and after breakfast we climbed back into our trucks to continue on toward the Front. We dropped off some of the men along the way and by late afternoon we arrived at Ist Division Head Quarters. We ate there and caught a much needed nap.

11

Part 11: Hurtgen Forest, the Battle of the Bulge, and Hill 587

We were awakened about three hours later and lined up to receive our combat equipment; helmets, rifles, bayonets, ammunition, grenades, packs, overcoats, a half pound block of TNT, blasting caps, the works. We then took another nap. We were wakened about 6:00 A.M., fed, then assembled to go to our Companies. I went back to "I" Company. When I arrived at "I" Company H.Q., the Company Commander remembered me. He said that he needed a second in Command for one of his squads.

I told him that I had been busted while away, but he told me not to worry about that because he needed me and he would take care of the necessary paperwork. I had to wait for someone from my squad to come get me, so the Company Commander and I talked, and he clued me into what was happening, which wasn't good. Later that morning the squad leader for the squad that I was to join appeared. We were introduced, he was fairly new from stateside, but had been in several battles since joining the 1st Division.

His name was Staff Sgt. Rogers. Rogers and I went to our squad so that I could get acquainted with the men, as well as our positions and objectives. It seemed as though it had been ages since I had left the Front but actually it had been only 39 days.

We were located a little east of Langerwehe, Germany in the Hurtgen Forest. Our main objective was to take the town of Langerwehe. It was cold, rainy and nasty. The Germans had plenty of artillery, which, they used night and day. The enemy was good at firing shells into the trees around us for tree bursts, which rained down on us from all directions. We all prayed that we would get through the trees and out into the open. Our planes couldn't fly in this weather, so it was up to us to move up as fast as we could without getting hit by small arms fire or artillery tree bursts. We did get pretty well out of the forest as we got close to Langerwehe, but one of our platoons got pinned down close to the town at what was called Frenz Castle. Our whole Company had very rough going until we bypassed the town, surrounded it, then finally we were able to capture and secure it. This was the last big battle before the 9th Division relieved us on December 7th.

After being relieved, the whole 1st Division moved to bivouac areas in the vicinity of Henri Chapelle, Belgium southwest of Aachen. We knew that this was another short rest, to get reorganized and re-equip for another major assault, which we would be clued in to in time. By December 9th, we were in our bivouac area. Our Company "I" ended up in a little village where our squad had two rooms over a cafe. There were eleven of us in the two rooms, sleeping in sleeping bags. We began to receive little pieces of information about what was ahead of us. We were to start training with the amphibious ducks, for the crossing of the Rhine River near Cologne. These things never happened, though, because while we were in rest, on December 16th or rather the night of December 16th the Germans began their "Big Offensive" that has become known as the "Battle of the Bulge".

On the morning of December 17th we were alerted to pack up and move out. There had been 700 to 800 German parachutists dropped in the general area of the Malmedy-Eupen Woods, a large forested area in

Belgium. We were taken by trucks to the forest where we spread out in a long line to comb the woods looking for the parachutists. Every 300 yards or so there was an open area called a firebreak. This is where I ran into MacGruer again.

As we walked along in a line through the woods we would push ahead of us deer, rabbits and even a few of the German parachutists. MacGruer was sitting in the firebreaks in his jeep and a 30 caliber machine gun mounted on it. He was all set to shoot deer, Germans, or whatever came out into the firebreak. We did capture several Germans and yes we did have several meals of fresh venison.

The second night out we got into a marshy area and spent a dreadful night sleeping on the bogs. I will not dwell on it but suffice it to say that it was very, very uncomfortable to try to sleep with a little snow on the ground, thick, thick, fog around us and the humps of peat bogs to try to sleep on! But, believe it or not it was going to get worse.

About December 19th, we were moved further south of Eupen to take up positions just behind the front lines just in case the Germans tried to break through that sector between Eupen and Malmedy. We had large supply dumps at Spa, Liege, and Verviers that the Germans needed very badly to help them sustain their huge offensive. Meanwhile during this time there were Germans in American uniforms, driving American jeeps and able to speak English with American accents, driving around behind our lines, trying to set up roadblocks at strategic intersections, making the situation extremely fluid. Most of them were caught without doing too much harm, but only because we were all exceptionally alert to the danger that they could and would cause. Security was beefed up during this time and passwords became essential. Passwords came down from 1st Division Headquarters and were changed daily. If we were moving about, such as going out on Patrol, we had to make sure that we had the latest password. The runners between Company H.Q. and the outlying platoons were always getting into trouble, even almost getting themselves shot.

Orders came down that we were moving over to guard a dam near Malmedy for a few days. We were also told to put any German souvenirs that we might have in our bedrolls at "I" Company H.Q. We found out later that a number of American G.I.'s taken prisoner by the 1st Panzer Division (German), southwest of Malmedy, were disarmed and then shot by their captors. Actually it had nothing to do with souvenirs at all. Anyway, this turned out to be an uneventful guard duty for about three days.

About December 24th we moved back just behind the Front lines to a Belgium farm. "I" Company H.Q.'s set up in the house and the rest of us bedded down in the out buildings. During the daytime we dug in our defenses and strung barbed wire with lookouts always on watch duty. Our platoon had the barn to sleep in when off duty. We had a fire going in an old 50 gallon drum so it wasn't too bad inside.

Christmas Day dawned clear and bright. This was the first day that we had seen the sun in quite a while. It had been foggy, with bone chilling dampness in the air. We were also glad to see the sun because the Allied Air Force came out and flew overhead bombing the endless German columns of tanks and men. For Christmas, we had hot food but nothing special and we didn't have to pull patrol duty, we just pulled our normal guard duty. The next few days brought more digging in and patrol duty. On December 30th we were told to draw lots for showers, I was one of the lucky ones who got to go for our showers.

The next morning we left our area in 4×4 trucks with tarps over the back, two truck loads of us. The weather had now turned cold, below zero and it was snowing. We had to drive about thirty miles to get to the showers. When we got there we found the showers in two large unheated tents, but the water was hot so we really enjoyed ourselves. On the way back to "I" company area that afternoon we ran into trouble because the password had been changed and guess what? We didn't know the new password. For all the MP's knew, we could be two truckloads of Germans.

After a few hours it got straightened out but we didn't get back to our area until about 12:30 A.M. When we were still a couple of miles from the farm where we were staying, we noticed a huge fire in the distance. As we drew closer we could see that it was the barn and house where we were staying, that was on fire. It seems as though a couple of men had come in from guard duty, and tried to build up the fire by pouring gasoline on it. The fire flamed up, the men dropped the gas can, which caught fire in the hay, etc. The whole barn went up quickly from that point, and also the house. I lost my pack, grenades, some ammo, etc. We couldn't even get close to the barn because of the grenades, bazooka shells, ammo, etc., were going off and exploding from all the heat. We were fortunate that we didn't attract some enemy artillery fire. We didn't have a place to sleep or blankets to keep us warm the rest of that night. The two men responsible were both from the Bronx, George and Jake (Jacob). Both were at the top of our list for extra duty from that time on.

The next morning, January 1, 1945, we moved out marching about seven miles that day to get to our new positions at the Front, where we were to be for the next few days. The snow was still falling and was about four feet deep in drifts and the cold had settled in to stay. The ground was hard so we carried half pound blocks of TNT, along with blasting caps to set it off. We finally arrived at our new positions in the early afternoon. Again I got lucky, as platoon H.Q. was in a farm house and all of the squad leaders and assistant squad leaders were able to stay at platoon H.Q. Our duty was to take out the patrols, to make contact with the enemy to try to find their positions, post the outpost guards at night, and supervise the work being done on the defenses, such as concertina wire. Most of the holes were already dug but we strengthened the roofs with more logs in case of enemy artillery fire and to keep the snow out.

During this time we had a contact patrol out that was late in coming back, we always tried to get back before daylight. Our squad was sent out to check on them. It was just breaking daylight when we got to our outpost. We saw some movement out in front of us so my squad moved out on our bellies to check it out. We found part of the patrol coming in but the rest had been killed in a firefight with the enemy. Only four of the men had even made it back that far, and two of them were wounded so that we had to help them back to the outpost. About the time that we arrived at the outpost, enemy artillery shells started landing in close to us so we all struggled back through the snow to our regular positions. That sure gets your adrenaline pumping.

A few days later, I was out supervising three men putting up concertina wire when someone hollered "halt!", then fired a shot that went through my pant leg about knee high. I hollered, "George was that you, you dumb New Yorker?" It was George, all right, the screw-up! We had a very serious talk about that, because all of the men in that area had been alerted to the fact that we would be out fixing wire in front of their positions.

January 14th I looked high and low for my St. Christopher medal that I had been carrying in my shirt pocket since August, when a French girl gave it to me. While I am not overly superstitious, I was upset about losing that St. Christopher medal. That day we received orders to move out the morning of January 15th. This was to be a full attack on the whole Front in order to straighten out the Front Lines once more. Our first objective was to take Hill #587, which, is somewhere between Butgenbach and Faymonville, Belgium. This would have been bad in any weather but the temperature was below zero, it was still snowing, the snow was waist high with drifts running up to five feet deep.

Late the afternoon of January 14th, I was informed that my squad had outpost duty that night. We ate a good hot meal that night, took a nap until about 11:30 P.M. when we moved out to the outpost to relieve the men who were on duty. We were wearing snowsuits as we called them, a trick that we had learned from the Germans. The Army had scrounged white sheets from the Belgium people for us to use to cover our dark clothes, which stood out in all that snow. Between the light snow falling and the cold, we spent a miserable night on outpost duty. It was quiet that night though, because there was no enemy patrol action in our area.

Just before daylight our Company came out through our outpost area and so began our attack on Hill #587 as our squad joined the rest of "I" Company. We had to change the lead scout often, because of the deep snow. One person could only break track for about twenty minutes in that deep snow. We soon ran into heavy small arms fire, but we were able to take our first objective, only to be pinned down by small arms fire from a hillside that was higher than our position. We had been able to take the hill because it wasn't completely light. Now that it was getting light we were like sitting ducks. We dug into the snow on that hillside looking for a way to escape the withering fire from the Germans. I was in a fairly good position but the squad leader sent back word for me to move up near him, so I moved up near him on my belly. He wanted to know what I thought we should do and I told him to dig in and stay put for a while. This answer wasn't good enough for him, he wanted me to move forward to check out the scouts. I told him I would go only if he went too.

We finally moved forward a few feet but as I went to his right there was a fence row that was just a little higher ground in front of me with the snow pretty well blown off it. The fence had been cut away, but as I tried to hurry over this area on my belly a rifle bullet hit me in the helmet, tearing the rim of the helmet loose, cutting my face, but the bullet missed the end of my nose and went into the ground.

I was stunned for a moment but quickly moved back behind the fence row dragging my rifle behind in my right hand by the stock end of the strap. Just as I was dragging my rifle over the fence row an enemy machine gun opened up on me hitting me in the right hand. It was just as though my right glove exploded, I didn't feel a thing at the time but could see right into the back of my hand, which had taken a short burst of five or six bullets.

  Now I really did dig and wriggle to get as low in the snow as I could behind that fence row. My head was beginning to throb, there was a huge knot on my forehead above and between my eyes. My right hand was bleeding profusely. I finally was able to get my left hand under me so that I could put my left fist inside my overcoat to put my thumb in the right armpit to try to slow down the flow of blood to my hand. I knew that I was on my own now, no one could get to me to help.

12

Part 12: Wounded Again on Hill 587

I heard the squad leader calling me, he had been hit in the elbow. I told him that I had been hit too, just dig in and wait because there was nothing that we could do now except wait! This all happened about 10:00 A.M. on January 15th. This was probably the longest day of my life as we lay there waiting, waiting, waiting!

During this wait there were things happening, enemy mortar shells were dropping in around us. The enemy had us under surveillance, and whenever the snow under me started melting I got wet and cold enough to shiver. The Germans would see movement on my part and would begin firing at me with small arms.

The bullets tore the pack on my back to shreds. Again I guess you could say that I was still lucky because along with 1/2 pound of TNT in my pack was at least two blasting caps. The bullets wouldn't hurt the TNT, but if they had hit one of the blasting caps, 'POW! This realization made me even more nervous than I already was.

Finally late afternoon came and with it came dusk. When I knew that the enemy couldn't see movement anymore I tried to move but I couldn't, I had lain there so long and gotten so cold that everything was stiff. At least the cold had helped my hand to quit bleeding, now if I could just get

PART 12: WOUNDED AGAIN ON HILL 587

to my knees. Slowly I moved a little, then a little more so that in a few minutes I was on my hands and knees. Now there was movement around me as some of the other men started moving, men from my squad.

    I told those who were able, to find all of the wounded and help them back to an aid station, especially T/Sgt. Rogers, our squad leader, who I knew was going to need help. After that, they were to report to Platoon H.Q., wherever that might be. I started walking back the way we had come that morning, and with the help from some of the Co. "I" men I made it back to the aid station. As I walked, my hand started bleeding again so I had to hold it bent up from the elbow and my left thumb putting pressure under my right arm. At the aid station they bandaged us up for travel, so that we could make it to the hospital. At the aid station I saw some of the men from my squad.

    In all I think that there were six of us wounded just from my squad. They had helped me take my pack off when we arrived at the aid station, the pack was riddled with bullet holes, but I kept my helmet, which had a huge gash right down the Big Red 1 painted on the front of it. I couldn't wear the helmet because of the big knot on my forehead, but I carried it anyway. Soon they had us patched up and loaded into ambulances for the ride to Liege.

    I arrived at the Liege Hospital sometime in the early morning hours. I was checked into a ward and finally could crawl into a nice warm bed. I was really beat, with very little sleep for the last thirty hours. The next morning I was examined and x-rayed by doctors who decided to operate on my right hand. That night about 10:00 P.M., I was taken to the operating room where I was given pentathol to put me to sleep and when I woke up it was morning and I was back in my bed. The nurse had awakened me to have my breakfast. That had been the best nights sleep I had in many days.

    Later that day we were moved by ambulance to a waiting train that took us to Paris. Why we ended up in the Paris Hospital, none of us could figure out. The bunks on the train were comfortable but it was hard to sleep with us all getting penicillin shots every four hours.

There were several "section 8" cases on board the train, some were genuine, many were not. Those that were genuine had battle fatigue or shell shock as they called it during WW1 and WW2. One man swept the aisle in our car all night long or at least all the way to Paris. Another man made noises like a locomotive including the whistles, all of the time. Another man just lay on his bunk with his eyes open, staring straight ahead. Another man just sat on his bunk groaning and moaning all of the time, with his head in his hands, he wouldn't answer anyone.

We finally arrived in Paris and were bussed to the Paris hospital. We settled in late that night ready for a good night's sleep. I swear I had only been sleeping for five minutes when they woke us up to get ready to move out. They bussed about thirty-five of us to the train station to catch another train to Cherbourg. The only good thing about the ride to Cherbourg is that we did get some sleep except for penicillin shots every four hours.

We arrived in Cherbourg that afternoon, and then we were bussed from the train to the harbor where we were loaded onto a small English boat to cross the channel back to England. I said that it was a small boat, a passenger boat I guess you would call it, but it was no ship. There were no bunks in this boat but we could use hammocks if we wanted to lie down. It took me several tries but I finally got into that hammock. It really wasn't too bad once I got into it and the boat got underway. I was sleeping shortly after we got underway, however, I did wake up when we got out into the channel because the boat was rocking and rolling but my hammock was just swinging back and forth putting me back to sleep.

We arrived in England sometime in the early morning mist, and tied up to a pier at Bournemouth, England. They had busses waiting for us as we left the boat, so we were bussed through Bournemouth and then out about six or seven miles to the hospital that would be our home for the next several weeks. We were all happy to be back in England again, as we all admitted. Europe didn't hold very dear memories for any of us.

13

Part 13: Recovery in England

A fellow that I met on the train between Paris and Cherbourg was in the same hospital ward with me, by the name of Al Sloniker, from Chicago. Another fellow in our ward was Marvin Stemwinder, that wasn't his real name but he went by that name because when he went to town, he didn't want the girls he met to know his real name. As it turned out, everyone called him by that name, even the nurses. I believe that he was from Alabama. There was also an Irishman from Massachusetts by the name of William French. There I also met Jimmie McDermit with whom I became friends, along with Al Sloniker. There were several other men in our ward who were a lot of fun and after what we had all been through, we wanted to enjoy everything. Almost everyone was always playing tricks on one another and just joking and having fun.

It was here that I met Kitty, the nurse. I was still getting penicillin shots every four hours. Kitty came into the ward to give me my shot early in the morning but she forgot the rule to always say our name when waking us up and I came up swinging and almost knocked her down. Kitty's Irish temper flared but she never ever forgot the rule again.

Sometime later, three or four days, she tried to pull the bandage off the back of my right hand without soaking it carefully. She tried to pull it off by jerking it as you would jerk tape off your skin that was stuck. The big problem was that my hand was healing so that when she jerked the bandage, it tore everything loose so that it really bled badly.

I grabbed the bandage from her and held it all together while yelling at Kitty to "get the hell out of my sight." I then walked up to the nurses station to get the bandage taped back on until the bleeding stopped. I had one of the nurses call my doctor, so that he could inspect the damage.

The doctor came in an hour or so later to check my hand. He soaked and removed the bandage, but wanted to know what I had been doing. I told him about Kitty jerking the bandage off my hand and the next time she came near me, I was going to tear her head off. The doctor told me that he would take care of it. I guess he did because Kitty was transferred to a different ward.

Several days later I was scheduled to have my hand operated on to do some clean-up work on it. I was given a shot of morphine about 45 minutes before going to the operating room. The morphine really went to my head. I walked up to the nurse's station, picked up a scalpel and proceeded to cut a piece of metal out of my little finger.

One of the nurses saw me, so with the help of a couple of men from my ward, they put me back to bed and took away my pajamas so that I wouldn't get out of bed. The orderlies soon came with a gurney to take me to the operating room.

Outside of the operating room was a waiting room for those who were waiting to be operated on. At this time I was given a local anesthetic to numb my hand. I was still a little high from the morphine but was slowly calming down. I lay there on that gurney waiting, and waiting until finally the man who was ahead of me finally was wheeled out of the operating room and it was my turn. It kept running through my mind, my turn in the barrel, my turn in the barrel. I guess it was the morphine still working.

In the operating room I was slid off the gurney onto the table and strapped down. I know that the doctor took some bullet fragments out as well as some bone fragments but I couldn't feel anything for a while. Finally, as the doctor worked I could begin to feel what he was doing.

The pain became more and more intense until I finally told the doctor that he had better give me another local. Instead he told me to hang on because he was almost through. He told the nurses to check the straps and keep me quiet. I only had a sheet over me but I was sweating profusely for what seemed like hours before he finally sewed up the back of my hand. I was soaking wet from head to toe.

Finally the straps were loosened and I was slid back onto the gurney for the trip back to the ward. When I got to my bed I was ready for it and I slept for several hours.

The days rolled along swiftly, we (Al, Jimmie, and I) made the trip into Bournemouth together a few times. They had some very good English bands at the tea dances in Bournemouth and we all enjoyed the music. We began to hear rumors that some of us might be going stateside.

A few days later it was confirmed that we really were going back to the States, home again! I had been overseas now for just over a year but it seemed as though it was much longer than that. So many things had been going on in my life in this past year.

14

Part 14: The Voyage Home on the Queen Elizabeth

We received our orders to be ready to move out in three days. Al, Jimmie and I were all going back to the States together. Three days later we were all loaded into buses for the trip to Bournemouth harbor and our waiting ship. What a ship it turned out to be, the Queen Elizabeth. We three ended up together in a "B" deck cabin. This was going to be like a cruise, and it actually did turn out great. The whole ship was turned into a hospital ship and they treated all of us wounded like Royalty. The food was great, and so for the next six days we enjoyed the Q.E., even the music played through the loud speakers was all "Big Band" music. We did get a little tired of "Don't Fence Me In" by Bing Crosby, especially the phrase "Give Me Land, Lots of Land". But all in all it was a great trip on a great ship.

The first day out of Bournemouth Harbor, a gambling hall was set up in a big room right up in the bow of the ship. Jimmie was one who loved to gamble but got seasick quite easily. Two days out of Bournemouth the seas got quite rough, even for a big ship such as the Q.E. About thirty minutes after Jimmie would go up to the "bow hall", I would go up to drag him and his winnings out of there. I only let him take about thirty dollars with him at a time. By the time that we reached New York, I was holding $350.00 plus a small pistol that he had won.

As we came closer to the East Coast, we again ran into the warm currents so we spent most of the time on deck in the sun. Early one morning we slowed and stopped to let the harbor pilot from New York come aboard. Then, we continued on slowly toward the New York harbor. Soon we were met by tugboats to help us into the harbor, then the "GREAT GREEN LADY" appeared (the Statue of Liberty) and we were met by dozens of boats of all sizes and types blowing their whistles and foghorns. The fireboats were spouting huge streams of water into the air. What a welcome committee for a bunch of homesick G.I.'s. This armada of boats escorted us all the way through Long Island Sound to our ship's berth in Manhattan.

It took us quite awhile to dock at our berth and then several hours to get ready and disembark into waiting buses for the ride through the Lincoln Tunnel to New Jersey and finally to Halloran General Hospital on Staten Island. We spent the next few hours getting settled, eating our evening meal, then talking about the last few days and the welcome we received coming into the harbor. We finally settled down in our beds, happy and tired, and we slept right through the thunderstorm that night.

The next morning we were all up early to get ready for breakfast. I don't know if the meals here at Halloran were really special, or if it was just being back in the States, but we all ate as though we hadn't eaten for a week. When we had all finished our breakfast we went back to our ward. About 9:00 A.M., we were all marched to a huge building with many cubicles. There we were interviewed in private to get our records verified, such as injuries, how long in the service, how long overseas, etc. This took several hours but by mid afternoon we had everything settled. We were informed that afternoon that we could have a 12 hour pass into New York City.

We, of course, jumped at the opportunity to see New York City. Al,

PART 14: THE VOYAGE HOME ON THE QUEEN ELIZABETH

Jimmy and I went on this pass together, we climbed aboard the Staten Island Ferry (5 cents) for the ride to Manhattan. There were two fellows from our ward on board the Ferry, so they joined us making a group of five of us to do the Big Apple together. When we arrived in Manhattan we decided to do some sightseeing first. We went to the Empire State Building, walked up Broadway, walked along the Battery, etc. We decided while we were walking around to have a hamburger or two, which we washed down with good old American beer.

We spent the day and the evening wondering around, just enjoying everything, we would stop to eat or drink a beer, then be off again. Time slipped away from us somehow and before we knew it the sun was coming up.

We had been having such a great time, that we had forgotten that we had been due back on Staten Island at 2:00 A.M. We headed for the Staten Island Ferry dock. By the time we docked on Staten Island, then walked back to Halloran General Hospital to check in, it was around 10:00 A.M., only a few hours late.

While checking in we found out that we were going to be moving out in a very short time. We did have time to shower and pack up, we then went to the Chow Hall to eat and then hurry back to our ward. By early afternoon we were lining up to board buses. This time the buses took us to Grand Central Railroad Station where we boarded a waiting train.

Once aboard the train and in the car to which we were assigned, Al, Jimmie and I, still together at this point and all tired, slipped off to sleep very quickly. When we awoke, we were moving along through the late afternoon dusk toward upstate New York. Somewhere in the vicinity of Albany, NY one car was dropped off. We then headed south into Pennsylvania, then west through Ohio and Indiana.

15

Part 15: Transport to Texas and Furlough Home

We were scheduled to go through Chicago but there were so many of us from the upper-midwest aboard this train, that the Army decided to head farther south through southern Indiana, Illinois, and into St. Louis. We stopped in St. Louis to let off two more cars, but the Army posted MP's all around our train so that no one could get off and disappear. The train started moving again after a couple of hours, we glided along through Missouri and into Arkansas where we had to stop because of water over the tracks.

  Our train was pulled onto a sidetrack, where we waited and waited, until we became bored. Several of us got off the train and walked to a little village close by. There was a bar in this little village but little else except a general store. The bar was none too clean so we decided to drink bottled beer. The barmaid was really something to behold, not too young, she wore a sack dress with no belt and was smoking a cigar. This was my introduction to the hills of Arkansas, actually, this was true for all of us because we were all from the upper-midwest. We only stayed long enough to drink the one bottle of beer and then headed back for the train.

PART 15: TRANSPORT TO TEXAS AND FURLOUGH HOME

We arrived back at the train in plenty of time. It was at least another half hour before we pulled out on the main track and started through the deep water. In a half mile or so, we pulled out of the deep water and started picking up speed toward Oklahoma, Texas, Arizona and into California. We played cards, told tall tales, slept and ate all the way into Los Angeles. These were Pullman cars that we were in, so we did have bunks to sleep in, but there had been quite a controversy over who would sleep in the top bunks. We had tried to make sure that the short men slept above, but that didn't work out in all cases.

In the morning while eating breakfast, the tall tales would begin about how badly each one had slept the night before. We soon arrived in L.A. to let off several cars and then continued east through southern Arizona, New Mexico and finally to El Paso, Texas where we were dropped off at Beaumont General Hospital at Fort Bliss. Fort Bliss is a regular Army Base with their own railroad siding right on the base, which is where we were delivered. We were then bused to the hospital.

It took us a few days to get situated, we were assigned to wards right away. Jimmie and I were still in the same ward, but we became separated from Al because he had some nerve damage. We were examined by several doctors to find out if they needed to do some immediate work on us. There were so many there that needed immediate attention, so the decision was made to let Jimmie and I have a 30 day leave to visit our homes. Since Jimmie lived in Detroit and I in Wisconsin, we decided to travel to Chicago together and then meet in Chicago on the way back to El Paso. We found out that because we were wounded veterans, we were eligible for passes on A.T.C. (Air Transport Command) and could fly into Chicago's O'Hare Field.

We left Fort Bliss Air Field for a flight into Roswell, New Mexico on a DC-7. From there we caught a flight going to the air base at Colorado Springs, where we arrived in the late afternoon. We checked on another flight out that night but we were told that it would be better to catch a flight in the morning. We were told that they had a transient barracks where we could sleep and go to the Mess Hall to eat.

    We checked into the barracks and cleaned up. We were just about to head out to the Mess Hall when several of the guys and gals from the air base showed up to ask us if we wanted to go to town with them, for their usual Friday night fling. We joined them and took one of the air base buses to town (Colorado Springs). We ate in town, had a few beers and had a pretty good time, then boarded the bus for the air base. When we arrived at our barracks, we slept for a couple of hours, then got up to watch the sun rise on Pikes Peak. As we watched it get lighter and the deep purple shades turn to reds and browns, I knew right then that I wanted to live close to the mountains someday.

    We left Colorado that day flying into Wichita, Kansas Air Base. We had several hours delay at Wichita, then finally flew out toward St. Louis and into a bad thunder storm, with rain squalls. It was already getting dark, partly because of the storm, when we approached St. Louis. When we came out of the clouds we were at about 500 feet and already half way down the runway so we had to circle around to get lined up again with the runway. Our hearts and our stomachs were right up in our throats before the pilot finally set the plane down and taxied up to the hangers. What a relief to be on the ground.

    We were escorted to the transient barracks, which was only a short distance from the hanger area. We cleaned up, ate at the local Mess Hall, then went back to our barracks to get some much needed sleep. Morning dawned fairly clear so that we were able to catch a flight out to Chicago's O'Hare Field. That flight was normal, and we were in Chicago by 11:00 A.M.

    Jimmie and I shared a taxi from O'Hare to downtown Chicago. I had to go to one train station and Jimmie went on to the Illinois Central Station to catch his train for Detroit. I was able to catch my train (The Milwaukee Road) with only a minimal wait. It took about three hours and forty-five

PART 15: TRANSPORT TO TEXAS AND FURLOUGH HOME

minutes to go from Chicago through Milwaukee and then on to Portage. I walked out of the Portage depot and started hitching a ride. It was no problem getting a ride in those days if you were in uniform.

   I arrived at home in Wyocena within an hour of getting into Portage. Many things had changed while I had been gone so it took me a few days to catch up on what was happening. I was very happy to be at home once more. Many of my old friends were away in the service but several were in the area. Toward the end of April I received a 30 day extension on my furlough, which meant that I wouldn't need to be back in El Paso until the first part of June.

   During my first few days back I ran into Doris Schave at Pardeeville, so we started dating occasionally. Doris and I were in Madison on May 8th, which was V.E. day (Victory in Europe). Now with the war over in Europe, we had to concentrate on Japan in the south Pacific. A few days after V.E. day my brother Vernon came home on furlough from the 82nd Airborne. We did celebrate when he came home.

16

Part 16: Rehabilitation at Beaumont General Hospital

Soon the end of May was getting close which meant that my furlough was almost over. I had to be back in El Paso by the end of the first week in June. Jimmie and I were to meet in Chicago so that we could return to El Paso together. We met at the Red Cross stand in the train station in Chicago. We had coffee and doughnuts at the Red Cross stand, then decided to do the town before we left. We ended up spending three days in Chicago before we finally got out to O'Hare Field to catch a plane out. We caught an A.T.C. flight from Chicago to Omaha.

    We stayed overnight in Omaha, then caught a flight to Wichita, Kansas where we caught a flight to Love Field at Dallas, Texas. We spent the night at Love Field hoping to catch a flight to El Paso, but our luck ran out. Now all of the strategic materials were moving toward the west coast. We kept getting "bumped" by these strategic materials so the next day we caught the Army Air Force bus into Dallas.

    Once in Dallas we went to the Greyhound bus station. We checked with Greyhound to find out what our bus fare would be into El Paso. We both had to wire home for money. Our money arrived in about two hours. Then, we bought our tickets and waited for the bus to arrive. Early in the afternoon we climbed aboard the Greyhound that would take us more than halfway across Texas and finally deposit us in El Paso.

We arrived back at Beaumont General Hospital only four days late. We were a little concerned about being late, but the Army decided to extend our furlough for the four days. We really weren't needed at the hospital because they decided not to operate on either Jimmie or I because there were so many other cases that needed more immediate attention.

Going into the Mess Hall to eat was a real experience. There were men all around us with their faces in various stages of construction or re-construction. Some of these men had been burned or had parts of their faces blown away or shot away. Some had no ears, some no noses, some no mouth. Many had to eat liquid food through a straw while their mouth and jaws were being rebuilt. Many had plates in their heads, or smooth skin where an eye should be. Eventually they would have an eye socket built for a glass eye. Some of the men carried pictures of what they were going to eventually look like when all of their re-construction work was done. Some of the men who were nearing completion on their faces looked very good. I guess some of those doctors were able to receive a lot of experience in re-construction. We, who only had superficial wounds, felt that we were very lucky.

Jimmie and I only spent about two or three weeks in the hospital area before we were transferred to the rehabilitation area where some openings became available. There were about five barracks in the rehab area but Jimmie and I ended up in different barracks. I became one of the barracks orderlies at my barracks. It really wasn't too bad because there were four of us, two kept up the latrines, and we other two kept the barracks in shape.

When the rest of the men fell out to their morning formation, we tidied up, then the rest of the morning was ours to do as we wished. We usually wrote letters and went to wash our clothes. In the afternoon, as soon as the other men fell out, we tidied up again, then went to the swimming pool to spend the afternoon. On Friday mornings we had to clean and wax the barracks floor, which took us most of the morning. Our biggest problem was monitoring some of the fellows who were slobs, so that they didn't leave a big mess when they fell out for the morning or afternoon.

In the evening we played cards, went to a movie at the Post cinema, or would go to El Paso. A few times we crossed the border into Juarez to go to the cockfights, which are legal in Mexico. When we went to the cockfights, we went in a fairly large group because those people take their cockfights very seriously. Those fights would last until the wee hours of the morning. We were very careful never to get into any trouble when over the border into Mexico.

17

Part 17: Final Transfer and Discharge

On August 15th the war ended in the South Pacific, which became V-J Day. A large group of us went to El Paso to celebrate. That turned out to be a wild night because everyone was celebrating. The police, the MP's, and ambulances were out in force that night trying to keep everything and everyone under control. I saw a large number of people hauled off by ambulance that night. Five of us men had to take a taxi back to the Post that night because the buses had stopped running at midnight. I think that it was around 1:30 A.M. when we finally checked in at the gate that night.

By the time that my birthday rolled around I was getting bored with El Paso, Beaumont General, etc. My birthday was on August 23rd and shortly after that, less that a week I think, the Army began to set up preliminary negotiations with us to get our impression on what it would take to discharge us from the Army. These negotiations went on for about a week, while we were all holding out for a substantial percentage of disability.

In the early part of September 1945, I received orders that I was being transferred to Percy Jones Hospital near Battle Creek, Michigan. I thought perhaps that Jimmie would be in the group going to Michigan but he was still at Beaumont General when I left there. Five of us men who were being transferred went into El Paso together and rented a car for the trip to Dallas. That turned out to be a fun trip, we drove straight through but changed off driving. We stopped to gas up the car and to eat but that was the only stops until we pulled into Dallas.

At Dallas we all went in different directions, except for one of the men and I were both going to Chicago. We caught a train at Dallas that was headed for Chicago. We both had a lot of sleep to catch up on, so the train was barely out of Dallas before we were sound asleep in our seats. That trip became a wee bit boring before we arrived in Chicago two days later. At Chicago we split up, as I was going on to Wisconsin for a three day delay, in route to Battle Creek, Michigan.

It was good to get home again, but I knew that I wouldn't be in the Army long now. After three days at home I headed for Battle Creek and Percy Jones Hospital. When I arrived at Percy Jones I was assigned to the Convalescent Section. Things here were a little more regimented, we fell out shortly after Reveille for roll call, then marched to the Mess Hall together.

After breakfast we would go back to our barracks until the morning formation at 8:00 A.M. The mornings were normally spent negotiating the details of our upcoming discharges.

In the afternoon we were given a list of activities that we could participate in. I picked motorcycle riding which turned out to be interesting. The first afternoon we spent changing oil and learning how to care for the motorcycles. The second afternoon we were allowed to start them up and ride to a field where we could ride them around to get better acquainted with them. These were old Army motorcycles, well used and with a good many eccentricities. The third afternoon we rode to an area where there were trails to ride on as though we were on a cross country course.

We all enjoyed these afternoon rides. We had to be back at our barracks

PART 17: FINAL TRANSFER AND DISCHARGE

by 4:30 P.M. because we had to stand the Retreat formation at 5:00 P.M. After retreat we were through for the day, and we could go to the Mess Hall to eat or go to the PX. In the evenings we played cards, shook dice or went to the Post movie theater.

The second week at Percy Jones we all began to see that we were getting down to the end of our discharge negotiations and by the end of the week we had the paperwork all completed. On October 6, 1945, we stood with our Discharge and separation papers in our hands, ready to be on our way home at long last.

THE END

Thomas E. French

Photographs

Pfc. Thomas French Wounded in Fight

Mr. and Mrs. Earl French of Wyocena have received a telegram stating that their son, Pfc. Thomas E. French was wounded in action on January 15th, in Belgium. He is now located in a hospital in England.

Pfc. Tommy French Is Home from Overseas

Mr. and Mrs. Earl French of Wyocena have received word from the War Department stating that their son, Tom, arrived home from overseas on March 19th, and was landed at Staten Island, N. Y., on that date. Tom was wounded in Belgium on January 15th, and was awarded the Purple Heart. He has been in a hospital in England until evacuated to be returned to this country.

He is expected to come home for a brief visit with his parents, but may be sent to a hospital in this country instead, in which case his mother will go to see him. The exact extent of his injuries is not known to his family.

PHOTOGRAPHS

Doris Schave French and Thomas E. French

PHOTOGRAPHS